TOP TIPS: WELCOMING SPECIAL CHILDREN

Denise Abrahall

Copyright © 2005
First published 2005
ISBN 1 84427 126 9

British Library Cataloguing-in-Publication Data.
A catalogue record of this book is available from the British Library.

Scripture Union, 207–209 Queensway, Bletchley, Milton Keynes, MK2 2EB, England
Email: info@scriptureunion.org.uk
Website: www.scriptureunion.org.uk

Printed and bound in Dorchester, England by Henry Ling.

Logo and cover design:
www.splash-design.co.uk

Scripture Union Australia
Locked Bag 2, Central Coast Business Centre, NSW 2252
Website: www.scriptureunion.org.au

Internal design:
www.splash-design.co.uk

Internal illustrations:
Colin Smithson

Scripture Union USA
PO Box 987,Valley Forge, PA 19482
Website: www.scriptureunion.org

The right of Denise Abrahall to be identified as author of this work has been asserted by her in accordance with the Copyright, Designs and Patents Act 1988.

Scripture Union is an international Christian charity working with churches in more than 130 countries, providing resources to bring the good news about Jesus Christ to children, young people and families and to encourage them to develop spiritually through the Bible and prayer.

As well as our network of volunteers, staff and associates who run holidays, church-based events and school Christian groups, we produce a wide range of publications and support those who use our resources through training programmes.

INTRODUCTION

We can thank God that we are all made differently and each of us has a unique place in his world. But what does that mean in reality when we talk about our church activities being accessible to all? The vast majority of people can walk into a church, learn about God's Word, worship and share fellowship. However, what about those whose intellectual understanding makes sermons meaningless, whose anxieties cause them to rush around or whose legs will not allow them to climb the steps to the front door? Is it possible to have an inclusive church where God's love will be demonstrated to all, a church where all are welcome and barriers to access are dismantled?

This book will give you some ideas and tools to make your church and its activities welcoming to children with special needs and their families, a place where all can learn about our amazing God.

NUTS AND BOLTS

What do we mean by 'special needs'?

The term 'special needs' is very broad and is used to describe needs that a child has, that will require extra help in one, or more than one, area. The term 'Special Educational Needs' has a legal definition. Children with special educational needs all have learning difficulties or disabilities that make it harder for them to learn than most children of the same age. These children may need extra or different help from that given to other children of the same age. This extra help may be needed because of a range of needs, such as in thinking and understanding, physical or sensory difficulties, emotional and behavioural difficulties, difficulties with speech and language, or how they relate to and behave with other people.

The special needs we encounter amongst the children we are working with might be temporary, like a child who has broken a leg or a child experiencing a bereavement. However, we generally think of special needs as being of a permanent nature, such as Down's syndrome which will affect learning, or physical disability, for instance, cerebral palsy. Many groups may include children with Dyspraxia or Attention Deficit and Hyperactivity Disorder (ADHD) where the children can be impulsive and lively.

All children with Autistic Spectrum Disorder, ASD, share a number of impairments, some more noticeable than others. They find it hard to understand and use non-verbal and verbal communication, and to understand social behaviour. This affects their ability to interact with children and adults. It is hard for them to think and behave flexibly, which may be shown in restricted, obsessional or repetitive activities.

Whether permanent or temporary we need to provide extra help to the individual with a special need. This may mean extra resources such as helpers, special equipment or ramps. More commonly it means extra care in adapting materials and activities to make them accessible.

Why do we need to think about this?

Each day more than 60 children are born or diagnosed with a serious disability. There are around 555,000 children/young people in the UK who have some form of disability and/or chronic illness.

Yet, as we look around most churches there tend to be fewer people with special needs than these statistics would suggest. This is a largely unreached group who need to be given opportunities to learn of a God who loves them so much that Jesus died for them. Jesus met people where they were. He shared stories with them and posed questions, giving time and space for all people to answer. He talked directly to people and physically touched them. Think of children who come into a church only to find that the talk is directed above their heads to 'able' people. These are the children who may feel separate, ignored or even mocked by others in their school, clubs or community. Of all places, church should be a very different and welcoming experience for them.

Often it is the attitude that underlies their welcome to church that makes someone with special needs decide whether or not to return, rather than difficulties with a step or the sound system. Frequently, families who have a child with a disability try numerous churches in search of a place where they feel accepted and where they may all be able to relax and worship without being judged! Many families have given up altogether on finding a church for the whole family. Family members take it in turns to stay at home with their child with a disability. Alternatively, parents never sit through a whole service because they always have to leave with their child to take them for a walk or join them in the children's group. There are so many battles for families with a child who has a disability, that the battle to find a church becomes one battle too many!

What is the Disability Discrimination Act?

It has often been the need to concur with new legislation that has driven churches to make premises, activities and services inclusive. We do indeed need to make sure that we make the Christian church truly open to all. But it would be wonderful if the secular world looked to churches to see how to be truly inclusive.

The Disability Discrimination Act (DDA) gives us a definition of disability as 'a physical or mental impairment, which has substantial and long-term adverse effect on a person's ability to carry out normal day-to-day activities'. It includes disabilities such as: severe disfigurement, impairments helped by artificial aids, progressive conditions and genetic predispositions.

The DDA states what our duties are. In brief:
• Since December 1996 it has been unlawful to treat a person less favourably because of their disability.
• Since October 1999 we have needed to make reasonable adjustments to the service we provide (for example, give extra help, change the way we do things, have written policies and procedures and provide auxiliary aids such as hearing loops).
• Since October 2004 we have needed to make reasonable adjustments to physical features such as doorways, steps and toilets. What we need to do will vary according to our resources, what we have to offer and the effect of disability on the individual child. We must be 'reasonable' in our decisions and actions. We can refuse to include certain people for health and safety reasons but we would need

to have clear, written reasoning for this and have tried to find a 'safe' alternative. We could also refuse entry to someone if their inclusion would lead to no service for others because of the costs, both financial and in staffing. We are able to offer a slightly different service if other options have been considered and this is the best option.

These duties laid out are both anticipatory and continuing. This means that we need to consider possible changes to be made, even if we do not yet need to or cannot alter things now for the current congregation. Who knows who will come along to church next Sunday with a special need we have not even considered?

It is important that we remember that the DDA covers children as well as adults and it makes no difference if it is volunteers providing a service (which is usually the case in churches). We are still expected to comply.

Attitude changing
- **_Treat with dignity and respect_**
In all we do, we need to think about dignity, equality and respect. Are we being respectful of all people, treating them equally? One church, trying to provide for a wheelchair-user put up a shower curtain instead of a door in one cubicle in the ladies' loos. This church member had been unable to shut the toilet door. This did enable her to use the toilet independently but does it cater for her dignity and respect?
- **_Don't rush to do everything_**
It is often easier and quicker to do something for someone else rather than give people time and opportunities to do it for themselves. How do we feel if things are always done for us and we are made to feel inferior? How do we learn about God if we are not given an opportunity to explore for

In reality...

A church in Bracknell appointed someone to co-ordinate the work with children with special needs who gathers useful information and then decides how best to include each child with a disability. Extra resources are made, bought or adapted. Helpers are drawn in and trained to give support. For example, a child with autism has a helper to sit with them at the back during worship time which allows the child to move around and worship in their own way. The helper goes with the child to the children's group and may stand at the back while the child watches or sits with them to do a puzzle. The helper may adapt the teaching to make it relevant and motivating.

ourselves? Jean Vanier, founder of L'Arche communities where people with disabilities live alongside non-disabled people, said: 'Loving someone is not about doing things for them but revealing to them that they are precious.'

In reality...

In a church in Guildford, it was decided that the main service was not catering for some children with special needs which meant that their families missed out too. They set up a monthly group for these children. Some families brought their children at the start of the service so that they could go into the main service to worship. Other families brought their child after the worship time.

- **Raising disability awareness**

Within our churches we all need to work towards disability awareness and to know about policies regarding welcoming children with special needs. If one of your helpers on Sunday were said to have been discriminatory towards a child with special needs the church leadership is held responsible. They should have ensured that all helpers have some understanding of disability.

- **Adjustments to the premises**

Usually this means practical, low-cost adjustments. We need to make all that we offer as inclusive as is possible with our available resources. A church with a larger congregation and income would be expected to make physical alterations that would not be possible or expected from a small church without the resources.

- **Seek out creative solutions**

A church could be seen to be discriminating if we treated someone less favourably because of a disability or if we were not complying with the duties listed in the DDA without justification. For instance, we would not be offering a service to someone who wanted to participate if they could not physically enter the building. What are the alternatives? Could people from church visit a disabled person at home or visit the local respite centre once a month to provide worship there? It is important to advertise adaptations made and available provisions.

It would also be viewed as discrimination if we made our service unreasonably difficult to use. For instance, do we insist that someone with a disability such as ADHD or ASD sits still and in silence for a long time?

Each case needs to be judged separately. Guidelines about general disability etiquette is in Part Three.

2

GETTING STARTED

What can we do to aid inclusion and welcome the group?

A church needs a policy on the inclusion of those with disabilities, so everyone is clear what needs to be done. An example of guidelines are in Part Three.

Inclusion within whole church activities

A whole church vision for making the church welcoming and accessible is needed. Try one or more of the following ideas.

- *Do some research*

Complete a questionnaire among families with a child or children with special needs. It might give you some surprising information.

- *Create an action plan*

See page 23

- *Set up an area for 'lively' children to use*
- *Remove everyday clutter* that could get in someone's way.
- *Appoint a coordinator*

Like the church in Bracknell, mentioned on page 8, appoint a coordinator who makes sure all children are included and maintains the priority of welcoming special children.

- *Build a team of helpers*
- *Raise disability awareness*

Everyone helping within your church needs some disability awareness. Once a year 'Through the Roof', an organisation that works to assist churches in becoming more accessible, provides resources to help to run a 'disability awareness' service. More detailed training on disability, especially on the specific disabilities of children within the church, would be valuable for those directly involved. This information will help them to understand and communicate with the children.

- **All-age worship**

Making activities inclusive for children with special needs will certainly make use of the principles of good all-age worship. Those seeking to include people of all ages will want to include those who could be excluded by their disability. For further details on *Top Tips: All-Age Worship*, turn to the inside of the front cover.

- **Think of the family during church time**

Take the initiative rather than wait for tired parents to do something: try a 'buddy' who sits alongside the child or encourage a general whole church responsibility for looking after church children. Or if a family prefers to sit in a particular place, reserve those seats for them so they do not need to get there early all the time. Families will feel happier to be in seats where they feel comfortable – seats where they can see, hear, are not segregated and maybe with or without distractions.

- **Think of the family the rest of the week!**

Some families can never get to social events because of difficulties with babysitters, or they are not invited to whole family events, or know these will be too difficult because of their child. Are there ways to help them not feel isolated and left out? Parents and siblings of children with a significant special need may have little or no time away from

In reality...

One church set up a support group for families, mums, dads and siblings. They were amazed at how keen families were to meet with others, whether at a coffee morning or evening social to chat, let off steam or to listen to an outside speaker talking about, say, benefits or schooling. Once comfortable with the group some people decided it was 'safe' to come along to regular church services and activities. One church is now one of the recognised providers of respite care in their town by running a club for children with special needs on a Saturday morning.

them. Can your church give them a short break, by organising activities just for siblings?

Inclusion in children's and young people's groups

There is no one pattern of inclusion that will work for all. Carefully and prayerfully consider how best to show God's love to each child. Look at their unique personality and find ways to make activities accessible to them.

Communication
*   Talk to parents/carers and gather information about the child – their likes/dislikes and particular abilities/difficulties, even visit them at home or if parents agree, contact their school to talk to the child's teacher. (See Part Three for a sample observation sheet and new child form.) Use this information to build up a concise written picture of the child to give those working with him/her an idea of what is best for the child. For instance, a child may need to be first at an activity, before all the other children, so as not to be overwhelmed by too much going on.
*   Provide training on disability for those involved in children's work. It's good for all to have some awareness of disability and the particular policies that your church has for welcoming these children.
*   Work as a team, discovering and communicating between children's workers and helpers on what is and is not working successfully. Share the workload if extra preparation is needed.
*   Build an environment where all children feel free to ask questions. This includes asking about how and why others are different. This will stimulate healthy conversation to help them value those who are different. Children's candid questions can be difficult but talk honestly with them.

- Too much spoken language can confuse. Children with a significant learning difficulty are likely to have a smaller vocabulary than their peers, so minimise the spoken message. Instructions should be short and simple, as should the teaching. One simple truth is enough for each session.
- Avoid the use of abstract ideas and metaphors when working with those with learning difficulties or ASD, as you would with younger children. These can be taken literally and create confusion. Jesus is the light!! The only way to God is through Jesus!! If you do use abstract concepts make sure that you explain them clearly to the children. There will be times when illustrations in the Bible need explanation.
- Some children need routine – ensure that they know what is about to happen. Give them a plan or a warning when the activity is about to end. Make sure that if a child needs their own seat each week, they can have it. This would be particularly helpful for children with ASD, with ADHD, or Dyspraxia.

Preparation
- Think specifically about each child when planning activities to ensure they are memorable and enjoyable. Some children, especially those with ASD, may be sensitive to sensory overload. Certain noises, busy environments, lighting and being touched may be difficult for them to cope with at times. Could things be done differently?
- Prepare each session with a range of abilities and learning styles in mind. We all have preferred ways of learning so make your sessions varied. It is generally accepted that we learn more by doing than hearing. Aim for high quality materials, bright paper, large boards and good writing equipment.
- Advanced planning means that additional materials can be found.

- Allocate responsibility to someone for making sure there will be material suitable for each child.
- Devise a way of allocating a 'buddy' to work with the children who need 1:1 help. For more information turn to page 20.

Creativity and flexibility

Be creative about adapting activities/ideas by thinking about the actual children in the group. This is the key to accessibility.

- Make your activities multi-sensory. This will help many children who might otherwise find concentration and understanding difficult. Have relevant and motivating things to look at, feel, listen to and maybe smell and taste. Label boxes of 'props' that you can use during different activities, like big clear pictures, puppets and small percussion instruments.
- Quietly give children with learning and physical disabilities options about joining in. They may be happy to watch at times, they may want to do the same as everyone else with help/unaided, or they may prefer to do something similar which they find easier.
- Give all children opportunities to join in activities. Although a child may not be able to speak, they could push a button to make something work, hold up a picture, or communicate using signs/gesture during a drama activity.
- Have a range of craft activities available. They can be on the same theme and age-appropriate but some may require less developed skills. If asking the group to draw a picture there may be an option of colouring one, or asking someone to draw something for them, or working in a pair. If making a mobile, particular jobs

could be allocated that are appropriate to the abilities of the group.
• Don't worry if all children are not engaged in group activities at all
times. Some children need more space and time out.
Sometimes it is better if a child does something different
with an adult elsewhere, rather than being in a group that
will make them anxious and potentially disruptive. It might
be appropriate for you to set up a 'safe' area where
children can go if they need space. Try to stay in the area of
the children's work so they can still hear and see what's
happening. This is important for child protection reasons too.

Practicalities
• Make sure that you are working somewhere that is physically
accessible. This includes making areas clutter-free (to avoid trip hazards
for those with visual impairment as well as those with mobility
difficulties) and ensuring surfaces are level and not slippery.
• Inclusion means being part of the group and not being apart from it
so have seating at the same height. Make 1:1 helpers a part of the
whole group too. Value participation at any level and avoid making a
child with a disability appear obvious.
• If a child has a hearing loss they need to sit near the front with the
leader's face clearly in view. Leaders should not have
their back to the light. If the loop system is available,
check that it is working. Try to reduce background
noise. (Carpeted floors help with this.) Be aware that
small group discussion can be difficult for children
with hearing loss.
• Think where a child with a visual impairment
should sit and how visual material is presented.
Some pictures may be too busy for some children.

Some children may need pictures/writing presented very close to them or to one side.

- Make teaching relevant by relating it to their experiences. For instance, in talking about sin you might talk about someone taking someone's CD. Children with learning disabilities have life experience according to their age although their understanding may be of younger years. Use their fascinations like Thomas the Tank Engine or spiders to provide examples of situations.

- Usually activities should be kept short because attention spans may not be long. Shorter activities on the same theme are generally best and there should be something to suit each individual during the session. However, for some children, leaving an activity before they are ready may be upsetting. If this is so, allow time to complete an activity while others move on.

- Some children may only be able to read at a low level or not at all. Some children with learning disabilities who read are very proud to be able to do so and should be given opportunities to use this skill at their level within the sessions. Others may feel embarrassed. When using written resources, have a simplified version using fewer words and age-appropriate pictures to help.

- Wherever possible, include children with their peer group.

Behaviour

- Display rules that the children have agreed on, making sure children are clear why these are good rules. Help them to know the consequences of breaking them. You must be consistent otherwise you will find the rules counterproductive. Make sure all helpers are aware of them.

- Expect good behaviour from all children but be tolerant of unusual behaviour. For instance, someone may be listening even though they are not looking at the speaker or even though they are doing something else the whole time. Some children may need to move about quite regularly. Understand that some unusual behaviour is part of the disability and not just 'naughty behaviour'. Move calmly and avoid shouting so that the children feel you are in control.
- Praise good behaviour and work. Reinforcing the good helps to reduce the need for attention-seeking behaviour as well as making children feel valued. If a child is displaying challenging behaviour, redirect them or change the activity. Make sure that you do this early or the child may think that unacceptable behaviour earns a reward. Some children need opportunities to expend some energy, so have exercise regularly interspersed with quieter activities. If children come to groups directly from the main service, organise a physical activity before they sit down.

At the end of this book there are 12 TOP TIPS that summarise some of the key points.

In reality…

A friendly, lively young man who had ADHD, was proving a challenge to those working with him in church. After consultation it was decided that he could take his Game Boy into his group as long as it was on 'Silent'. So he joined in with the others, answering questions and listening whilst playing his Game Boy. (Generally those with ADHD are great multi-taskers.) Soon there was amazing evidence of the growth of his relationship with God. One day, this young man in a school RE lesson talked about the graphic of the three-arrowed recycling symbol and said it was 'like God, through Jesus pouring his love into us, so that we can pour it out to our friends, and then back to God in praise.' He had almost been excluded from his group at church!

Making things multisensory

- Use **visual material** to help children who find too much spoken language difficult to process. For instance, puppets capture attention and aid imagination, as well as bringing spoken words to life. Think about the size of puppets so that they can be easily seen but are not frightening. Carefully chosen pictures, posters and photos help to make spoken language clearer. Simple felt flannelgraphs, magnetic boards or Velcro boards, with character and object shapes, are simple to use and are cheap and portable.
- When talking to children use **gesture and big body language**. This gains attention and gives understanding. If someone in your church knows sign language, use them. Sign language helps those with learning difficulties as well as those with hearing impairments and everyone else too!
- Use **objects and tactile aids** with children with visual impairment and/or profound disability. Objects that cue them into activities can be used to let them know what is happening, like a tambourine given to them when it is time to sing. You could have an object that the child can hold when you talk about Jesus and thus they come to associate this object with Jesus. (But do ensure that you explain that the object is not Jesus!) Use tactile books with different surfaces to explore.
- **Craftwork** may be tactile or use different smells. Be creative. If Mum uses a certain perfume, this could be what is used to associate with her. What smell could you use to signify God who is love?
- Building **story boxes** to go with Bible stories will bring stories alive. For instance, a box made for the story of Noah could include a hammer, wood and maybe nails, a boat, people, pairs of various animals, water spray, a bird, a leaf and a globe. When the story is told, the props could be used as visual aids to involve the children.

- Many children with learning disabilities enjoy **music,** and for some it is easier for them to learn information through song. For instance, it has been found that many children with ASD learn better if the information is put to a rhythm like a rap. When it is time to worship, some may just 'sing' and find actions difficult, others may play an instrument such as a tambourine or wave a flag. Action songs encourage participation even if children cannot sing well. With older children, make action songs age-appropriate, perhaps using recognised signs from British Sign Language or Makaton.

- Using **food** can make Bible stories more memorable and provide aids to learning for children. For instance, when telling of the feeding of the 5,000, share some fish and bread to smell and taste. Make sure you know if anyone has food allergies.

- There are times in the Bible that illustrate the importance of **human touch**. Jesus touched people who would have been shunned by society. Think if touch could be used to illustrate your session. For instance, could group members wash each other's feet like Jesus washed the feet of his disciples? Do what is appropriate but bear in mind child protection issues when thinking of activities involving touch. We need to ensure the children are comfortable, and leaders not in a position where any allegations can be made against them.

> **In reality...**
>
> I recently visited a church where the young people had made things to go into story sacks for younger children, giving them an opportunity to serve as well as utilising their amazing creativity. Although they had designed their story sacks for younger children, they may just as well have been for those with disabilities.

Setting up a buddy system

Look for caring and compassionate volunteers who are interested in special needs issues. They should be good at working with children and young adults and need to be flexible and imaginative. Write a job description for potential buddies and make sure everyone knows the extent and limits of their responsibilities. Give opportunities for new buddies to sit in on a Sunday morning session to get to know the child and understand his/her specific needs. Make sure children's group leaders are aware of the child's needs and understand the role of the buddy. It may help to use speakers from outside the church to train leaders and buddies regarding disability issues.

Not all children with a disability will need a buddy. Some may be quite independent, needing only a little additional support from a group leader. For some teenagers the cell group structure may be very effective, with other members of the same age supporting the disabled teenager. For those children who you feel need support, set up a rota so that each buddy works with the same child for one or two Sundays per month. If there are several children with special needs in your church nominate one team member to be responsible for all administration and coordination.

The buddy:

- Is caring and compassionate.
- Is responsible for one or two children.
- Always works with the same children to get to know them.
- Befriends the child and family so is able to support them more successfully.
- Learns about the needs of the child and is aware of health issues.

- Seeks advice from the child's parent about dietary and toileting needs. This is most important.
- Learns fire evacuation procedures and practice, especially if the child uses a wheelchair and access is difficult.
- Is willing to mediate between group leaders and parents to discuss the best ways to support the child in the group.
- Adapts teaching materials in advance to meet the child's needs.
- Helps the child make friends with others in the group.
- Helps the group understand and tolerate inappropriate or unusual behaviours.
- Does not speak for the child or do things for them unless really necessary.
- Treats the child in an age-appropriate way, whatever their ability
- Doesn't talk about the child to others when they are present and always includes them in the conversation.
- Allows the child to voice opinions and preferences as much as they are able.
- Prays for the child. Asks the parents what to pray for. Doesn't pray for healing without first asking them.

How do we know that the children are learning?

For some children we might never know much about their relationship with God. For some, their faith might be limited to knowing that God loves them, disabilities and all. This knowledge can and has brought about changes in the lives of many, that are obvious to those close to them. Some children will never be able to make a verbal or 'reasoned' response, as this necessitates more intellectual understanding and communication skills than they have. Faith is not about intellectual understanding. Faith transcends academic abilities.

There are many stories of people with learning disabilities who have been included within the church community and have become happier, less anxious and frightened, more communicative and actively involved in the church family.

12 top tips on welcoming special children

1. *Be focused* – on the children first and then their disabilities.
2. *Be a team* – use your gifts/skills.
3. *Be flexible* – with activities, groupings, organisation, and teaching.
4. *Be resourced* – make the best use of people and materials.
5. *Be multi-sensory* – to engage/illustrate/emphasise/motivate.
6. *Be clear and relevant* – avoid the abstract and metaphors, use simple, concise language.
7. *Be informative* – have a routine and be clear about what's happening.
8. *Be aware* – of impairments of those in the group and their effects.
9. *Be big* – use body language and exaggerate.
10. *Be accessible* – attitudes, physically, academically.
11. *Be discreet* – include by mixed ability planning so children's disabilities won't be obvious.
12. *Be expectant* – of good behaviour.

PRACTICAL POSSIBILITIES

3

General disability etiquette

- View the child with a disability as a person, not a disability.
- Do not condescend.
- Be courteous.
- Offer assistance, but ask before acting.
- Don't pretend obvious disabilities don't exist.
- Speak directly to the child.
- Treat the child as if they are healthy. Having a disability does not mean they are ill.
- Don't judge lack of response as rudeness or lack of understanding.
- Take care not to startle the child.
- Relax and enjoy the child's company.

Guidelines

Sample Action Plan for including children with special needs:

In order to ascertain how we can best meet the needs of all children we will consider each child individually, trying to find ways to include them wherever possible. A systematic approach to maximise successful inclusion and lessen distress, is taken.

As a child with special needs comes into the church we will:

Speak with parents/carers about their child, gathering information and putting it onto an information sheet, to be kept in the child's records. There is a standard information sheet in order to ensure that all necessary data is gathered, but additional material can be added.

1. A children's worker or youth worker will observe the child in a familiar setting with the parents' agreement. This may be at home or at

school. This will build a rounder picture of the child and their personality. They will also find some basic information on the child's disability if they have a diagnosis.

2. A team of children's workers/youth workers/relevant people from church will discuss the child and make a decision about whether the child can be included. All possible ways of inclusion should be considered and only if it is totally unmanageable will access to activities be denied. If a child cannot be currently included in existing activities, other ways of helping the child to hear the gospel should be considered. Ways to remedy the current difficulties with inclusion should also be sought, so that the child can later participate.

If it is decided to include the child, then the following steps need to be taken:

3. A key person is to be nominated as a contact person regarding the child and coordinating plans for their inclusion. This person is the bridge to the family, building trust, working with them and offering them manageable support.

4. How best to include the child should be discussed so that realistic plans can be drawn up. For instance, will the child need a helper, for how much and how long? Will they need this person to themselves? Is there enough help for the child to attend every week or only fortnightly?

5. The child should be allocated to a group and wherever possible this should be their peer group. Decide who will gather and adapt resources.

6. A group of children's workers, the group leader and any other relevant people should brainstorm ideas of how best to include the child in ways which value the child's input, are relevant to the child, and help them to

understand and avoid anxiety. Guidelines and training materials could be kept in a folder marked 'Special Needs'.

7. Think ahead to your next few sessions and how you can make them relevant to the child.

8. You may need to write a plan to help manage a child's behaviour, to avoid them becoming distressed and their behaviour consequently disrupting the whole group.

9. Seek helpers and identify their training needs. Use information resources you have, people within the church and the parents if that is suitable. (Note: parents need to feel their child is valued just as they are, and will welcome your help, but not if it means lots more work for them.)

10. Write a provisional rota for helpers.

11. Invite the child to come to an activity, preferably with a parent/carer for the first (or first few) times to help them settle. Observe one of their first sessions and record this on a standard sheet that can inform you to make changes and adapt as necessary.

12. Once the child and helpers have settled in, review how things are working and make necessary changes.

13. Work as a team, helping one another and learning together.

At Church:

1. We will seek to include all children/young people who would like to participate in church activities. To this end we will look at the possible ways access could be made available for individuals we cannot easily accommodate, with current physical access, activities and staffing.

2. We will plan ahead and look at potential barriers to understanding and participation, and address these as far as possible.

3. We will seek to make everyone working with children and young people aware of disability issues, and sources of information to assist them in this area.

4. We will respect and value all children for their individuality and what they bring to the group and church.

5. We will strive to make every child feel a valued group participant by giving positive feedback, reinforcing the things they do well and their good behaviour.

6. We will not discuss children and their disabilities in front of them unless they are comfortable with and active in the conversation.

7. We will encourage children to accept and value all children.

8. We will not ridicule or patronise anyone because of his or her disability.

9. We will prepare each session with a range of abilities in mind.

10. We will seek all possible ways to include all children in all activities, through flexibility, tolerance and adapting ideas and activities to make them accessible.

11. We will have a range of craft activities available to suit differing abilities.

12. We will help children with learning difficulties to understand rules, activity/timetable structure and the content of our sessions.

13. We will have reasonable expectations of all children and their behaviour.

14. We will gather as much information as possible about individual children, from parents/carers/school, about their likes/dislikes, strengths/weaknesses and particular needs.

15. Through discussions with parents/carers we will strive to find an appropriate and manageable way to include their child. Whenever

possible, this will be with the child's peer group.

16. We will seek to provide 1:1 support for children who need extra help because of disabilities or who are exhibiting challenging behaviour, through adult members, or where appropriate a younger 'buddy'. For those children and young people who need 1:1 support this may necessitate participating at allocated times when the support is available (for example, every other session).

17. We will use 'special interests' and fascinations positively to motivate and to encourage.

18. We will ensure that children with hearing loss and visual impairment are sitting near the front with the leader's face in clear view, visual materials clearly presented and background noise minimised.

19. We will strive to make our environment clutter-free, clearly labelled and set up to allow as much independent mobility for individuals with varying disabilities as possible, in the setting available.

20. We will ensure that support workers are aware of medical needs and that a record is kept of medication given, noting: medication; time; quantity and initialled by support worker and team member.

21. We will never encourage children to make a response to God until they are ready.

Sample forms

In creating your own forms you will need to include the following information.

Sample new child form

Name: DoB:

Address: Names of parents/carers:

Names of brothers/sisters: Other significant people:

School attended: Particular interests:

Particular dislikes:

Please tell us about any strengths and weaknesses that your child has that might best help us to include him/her.

Does your child have a medical diagnosis? If yes please state.

Does your child have any specific medical needs or allergies or intolerances?

Do you have any tips for us working with your child (like ways of best engaging your child, using gesture/signs or ways to avoid them becoming distressed)?

Please give us two phone numbers in case we have to contact you urgently.

Sample observation form

Name: DoB:

Date of observation: Group and leader:

Diagnosis and medical needs: Social skills:

Socialising with others: Joining in activities:

Any distress: Attention span:

Behavioural difficulties: Motor skills:

Gross (eg moving around):   Fine (eg pencil skills):

Feeding skills: Language skills:

Expression: Comprehension:

Sensory impairments: Response of adults to child:

Response of peers to child: Parental aims and preferences:

Action needed:

Contacts and books

Websites

- www.scriptureunion.org.uk/enable – Scripture Union's web pages designed to help children's workers in churches to be inclusive.
- www.throughtheroof.org – Working with churches for inclusion and raising awareness – has links to other sites.
- www.prospects.org.uk – Organisation that helps adults with learning disabilities know God.
- www.parenting.org.uk – Secular organisation offering information about disabilities and resources in a simple way.
- www.cafamily.org.uk – Information on conditions and support to families.
- www.signsofgod.fsnet.co.uk – Christian network of BSL signers.
- www.deafchristian.org.uk – Christian Deaflink UK.
- www.pastornet.net.au – Information on planning a worship service for Inclusion Sunday.
- www.cathchild.org.uk – Disability awareness activities that can be used with young people.
- www.drc-gb.org – Disability Rights Commission with information on Disability Discrimination Act.
- www.lichfield.anglican.org – 'Open to All' policy document produced in response to Disability Discrimination Act.
- www.kidshealth.org – Simple information for children/young people about disabilities.
- www.widget.com – Producers of 'Writing with Symbols' software – illustrates words with simple pictures.

Books about disability and the church

- Simon Bass, *Special Children Special Needs*, Church House Publishing, 2003 (0 7151 49997): simple and practical information on how to integrate children with special needs in a church setting.
- Kathleen Deyer Bolduc, *A Place Called Acceptance*, Bridge Resources, 2001 (1 57895 098 8): a useful practical book.
- Faith Bowers, *Treat with Special Honour*, The Baptist Union, 1997 (1 89807 708 8): evangelism and disability.

- Brett Webb-Mitchell, *Dancing with Disabilities*, The Pilgrim Press, 1997 (0 82981 152 4): lots of personal stories.
- Gene Newman, Joni Eareckson Tada, *All God's Children*, Zondervan, 1993 (0 31059 381 6): practical guide.
- Henri J M Nouwen Adam, *God's Beloved*, Orbis Books, 1997 (1 57075 133 1): how time with people with disabilities changed the author.
- Marshall Stewart Ball, *Kiss of God*, Health Communications Inc, 1999 (1 55874 743 5): written by a severely disabled boy.
- Jean Vanier, *Followers of Jesus*, Gill and Macmillan, 1993 (0 7171 2057 0): by the founder of L'Arche communities.
- Susan Murrell, *Worship ASAP*, Church House Publishing, 2003 (0 7151 4005 1): 40+ pick-up-and-use collective worship ideas for children with special needs.
- Liz O'Brien, *Connecting with RE – RE and faith development for children with autism and/or severe and complex learning disabilities*, Church House Publishing, 2002 (0 7151 4984 9).

- THE SIGNALONG Group – *Signalong Being With God, Signs for Christian Worship*, SIGNALONG Group, 2003 (1 902317 83 1).

Books for young people with learning disabilities
- Scripture Union, *What Jesus Did*, Scripture Union 2003 (1 84427 005 X): a look at the person of Jesus – teacher notes on the website to give ideas of how to use the book www.scriptureunion.org.uk/enable.
- Scripture Union, *What the Bible Is*, Scripture Union 2005 (1 84427 136 6): a look at what the Bible is.
- Scripture Union, *Bible Prospects* series 2005 (1 84427 066 1; 065 3; 064 5; 063 7): a series of four easy-to-read Bible reading notes.
- Jean Vanier, *I meet Jesus*, Paulist Press, 1987 (0 8091 2725 3): parts of the Bible simplified with black and white illustrations.
- Books by Build (Baptist Union Initiative with people with learning disabilities): *The Church, Joining the Church, Knowing Jesus, Following Jesus, Friends of Jesus*. Available from Baptist Union via website www.baptist.org.uk.

We know that God values each person. He showed this clearly through Jesus. Whether or not we see the children with special needs in our care respond to God during the time they are with us, we continue in faith, trusting that their relationship with Jesus is developing and growing. Enjoy your time with the children, learning from them as you try to help them learn, and you will discover the privilege of welcoming special children.